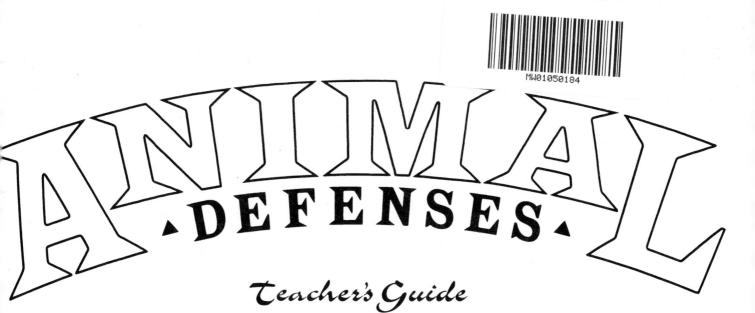

ANIMAL DEFENSES

Teacher's Guide

Grades Preschool–K
(can be modified for Grades 1–2)

Skills
Observing, Comparing, Communicating,
Identifying, Creative Thinking,
Using Scissors (optional)

Concepts
Protection, Predator-Prey

Themes
Systems & Interactions, Models & Simulations,
Scale, Structure, Diversity & Unity

Nature of Science and Mathematics
Real-Life Applications

Time
One 45-minute session
and
One 20-minute session

Jean C. Echols

LHS GEMS

Great Explorations in Math and Science (GEMS)
Lawrence Hall of Science
University of California at Berkeley

Illustrations
Carol Bevilacqua

Photographs
Richard Hoyt

Lawrence Hall of Science, University of California,
Berkeley, CA 94720. Chairman: Glenn T. Seaborg;
Director: Marian C. Diamond

Publication was made possible by grants from the A.W.
Mellon Foundation and the Carnegie Corporation of New
York. This support does not imply responsibility for
statements or views expressed in publications of the GEMS
program. GEMS also gratefully acknowledges the contri-
bution of word processing equipment from Apple Com-
puter, Inc. Under a grant from the National Science
Foundation, GEMS Leader's Workshops have been held
across the country. For further information on GEMS
leadership opportunities, please contact GEMS at the
address and phone number below.

International Standard Book Number: 0-924886-88-9

COMMENTS WELCOME

Great Explorations in Math and Science (GEMS) is
an ongoing curriculum development project. GEMS
guides are revised periodically, to incorporate
teacher comments and new approaches. We
welcome your criticisms, suggestions, helpful hints,
and any anecdotes about your experience present-
ing GEMS activities. Your suggestions will be
reviewed each time a GEMS guide is revised.
Please send your comments to: GEMS Revisions,
c/o Lawrence Hall of Science, University of
California, Berkeley, CA 94720. The phone number
is (510) 642-7771.

♻ Printed on recycled stock.

Great Explorations in Math and Science (GEMS) Program

The Lawrence Hall of Science (LHS) is a public science center on the University of California at Berkeley campus. LHS offers a full program of activities for the public, including workshops and classes, exhibits, films, lectures, and special events. LHS is also a center for teacher education and curriculum research and development.

Over the years, LHS staff have developed a multitude of activities, assembly programs, classes, and interactive exhibits. These programs have proven to be successful at the Hall and should be useful to schools, other science centers, museums, and community groups. A number of these guided-discovery activities have been published under the Great Explorations in Math and Science (GEMS) title, after an extensive refinement process that includes classroom testing of trial versions, modifications to ensure the use of easy-to-obtain materials, and carefully written and edited step-by-step instructions and background information to allow presentation by teachers without special background in mathematics or science.

Staff

Glenn T. Seaborg, Principal Investigator
Robert C. Knott, Administrator
Jacqueline Barber, Director
Cary Sneider, Curriculum Specialist
Katharine Barrett, John Erickson, Rosita Fabian,
Kimi Hosoume, Linda Lipner, Laura Lowell,
Carolyn Willard, Staff Development Specialists
Jan M. Goodman, Mathematics Consultant
Cynthia Ashley, Administrative Coordinator
Gabriela Solomon, Distribution Coordinator
Lisa Haderlie Baker, Art Director
Carol Bevilacqua and Lisa Klofkorn, Designers
Lincoln Bergman and Kay Fairwell, Editors

Contributing Authors

Jacqueline Barber
Katharine Barrett
Lincoln Bergman
David Buller
Fern Burch
Deborah Calhoon
Linda De Lucchi
Jean Echols
Alan Gould
Sue Jagoda
Robert C. Knott
Larry Malone
Gay Nichols
Cary I. Sneider
Elizabeth Stage
Jennifer Meux White

Reviewers

We would like to thank the following educators who reviewed, tested, or coordinated the reviewing of this series of GEMS materials in manuscript form. Their critical comments and recommendations contributed significantly to these GEMS publications. Their participation does not necessarily imply endorsement of the GEMS program.

ARIZONA

David P. Anderson
Royal Palm Junior High School, Phoenix

Joanne Anger
John Jacobs Elementary School, Phoenix

Cheri Balkenbush
Shaw Butte Elementary School, Phoenix

Flo-Ann Barwick Campbell
Mountain Sky Junior High School, Phoenix

Sandra Caldwell
Lakeview Elementary School, Phoenix

Richard Clark*
Washington School District, Phoenix

Kathy Culbertson
Moon Mountain Elementary School, Phoenix

Don Diller
Sunnyslope Elementary School, Phoenix

Barbara G. Elliot
Tumbleweed Elementary School, Phoenix

Joseph M. Farrier
Desert Foothills Junior High School, Phoenix

Mary Anne French
Moon Mountain Elementary School, Phoenix

Leo H. Hamlet
Desert View Elementary School, Phoenix

Elaine Hardt
Sunnyslope Elementary School, Phoenix

Walter Carroll Hart
Desert View Elementary School, Phoenix

Tim Huff
Sunnyslope Elementary School, Phoenix

Stephen H. Kleinz
Desert Foothills Junior High School, Phoenix

Alison Lamborghini
Orangewood Elementary School, Phoenix

Karen Lee
Moon Mountain Elementary School, Phoenix

George Lewis
Sweetwater Elementary School, Phoenix

Tom Lutz
Palo Verde Junior High School, Phoenix

Midori Mits
Sunset Elementary School, Phoenix

Brenda Pierce
Cholla Junior High School, Phoenix

Sue Poe
Palo Verde Junior High School, Phoenix

Robert C. Rose
Sweetwater Elementary School, Phoenix

Liz Sandberg
Desert Foothills Junior High School, Phoenix

Jacque Sniffen
Chaparral Elementary School, Phoenix

Rebecca Staley
John Jacobs Elementary School, Phoenix

Sandra Stanley
Manzanita Elementary School, Phoenix

Chris Starr
Sunset Elementary School, Phoenix

Karen R. Stock
Tumbleweed Elementary School, Phoenix

Charri L. Strong
Mountain Sky Junior High School, Phoenix

Shirley Vojtko
Cholla Junior High School, Phoenix

K. Dollar Wroughton
John Jacobs Elementary School, Phoenix

CALIFORNIA

Carolyn R. Adams
Washington Primary School, Berkeley

Judith Adler*
Walnut Heights Elementary School, Walnut Creek

Gretchen P. Anderson
Buena Vista Elementary School, Walnut Creek

Beverly Braxton
Columbus Intermediate School, Berkeley

Dorothy Brown
Cave Elementary School, Vallejo

Christa Buckingham
Seven Hills Intermediate School, Walnut Creek

Elizabeth Burch
Sleepy Hollow Elementary School, Orinda

Katharine V. Chapple
Walnut Heights Elementary School, Walnut Creek

Linda Clar
Walnut Heights Elementary School, Walnut Creek

Gail E. Clarke
The Dorris-Eaton School, Walnut Creek

Sara J. Danielson
Albany Middle School, Albany

Robin Davis
Albany Middle School, Albany

Margaret Dreyfus
Walnut Heights Elementary School, Walnut Creek

Jose Franco
Columbus Intermediate School, Berkeley

Elaine Gallaher
Sleepy Hollow Elementary School, Orinda

Ann Gilbert
Columbus Intermediate School, Berkeley

Gretchen Gillfillan
Sleepy Hollow Elementary School, Orinda

Brenda S.K. Goo
Cave Elementary School, Vallejo

Beverly Kroske Grunder
Indian Valley Elementary School, Walnut Creek

Kenneth M. Guthrie
Walnut Creek Intermediate School, Walnut Creek

Joan Hedges
Walnut Heights Elementary School, Walnut Creek

Corrine Howard
Washington Elementary School, Berkeley

Janet Kay Howard
Sleepy Hollow Elementary School, Orinda

Gail Isserman
Murwood Elementary School, Walnut Creek

Carol Jensen
Columbus Intermediate School, Berkeley

Dave Johnson
Cave Elementary School, Vallejo

Kathy Jones
Cave Elementary School, Vallejo

Dayle Kerstad*
Cave Elementary School, Vallejo

Diane Knickerbocker
Indian Valley Elementary School, Walnut Creek

Joan P. Kunz
Walnut Heights Elementary School, Walnut Creek

Randy Lam
Los Cerros Intermediate School, Danville

Philip R. Loggins
Sleepy Hollow Elementary School, Orinda

Jack McFarland
Albany Middle School, Albany

Betty Maddox
Walnut Heights Elementary School, Walnut Creek

Chiyomi Masuda
Columbus Intermediate School, Berkeley

Katy Miles
Albany Middle School, Albany

Lin Morehouse*
Sleepy Hollow Elementary Schoool, Orinda

Marv Moss
Sleepy Hollow Elementary School, Orinda

Tina L. Neivelt
Cave Elementary School, Vallejo

Neil Nelson
Cave Elementary School, Vallejo

Joyce Noakes
Valle Verde Elementary School, Walnut Creek

Jill Norris
Sleepy Hollow Elementary School, Orinda

Janet Obata
Albany Middle School, Albany

Patrick Pase
Los Cerros Intermediate School, Danville

Geraldine Piglowski
Cave Elementary School, Vallejo

Susan Power
Albany Middle School, Albany

Louise Rasmussen
Albany Middle School, Albany

Jan Rayder
Columbus Intermediate School, Berkeley

Masha Rosenthal
Sleepy Hollow Elementary School, Orinda

Carol Rutherford
Cave Elementary School, Vallejo

Jim Salak
Cave Elementary School, Vallejo

Constance M. Schulte
Seven Hills Intermediate School, Walnut Creek

Robert Shogren*
Albany Middle School, Albany

Kay L. Sorg*
Albany Middle School, Albany

Marc Tatar
University of California Gifted Program, Berkeley

Mary E. Welte
Sleepy Hollow Elementary School, Orinda

Carol Whitmore-Waldron
Cave Elementary School, Vallejo

Vernola J. Williams
Albany Middle School, Albany
Carolyn Willard*
Columbus Intermediate School, Berkeley
Mary Yonekawa
The Dorris-Eaton School, Walnut Creek

KENTUCKY

Joyce M. Anderson
Carrithers Middle School, Louisville
Susan H. Baker
Museum of History and Science, Louisville
Carol Earle Black
Highland Middle School, Louisville
April B. Bond
Rangeland Elementary School, Louisville
Sue M. Brown
Newburg Middle School, Louisville
Donna Ross Butler
Carrithers Middle School, Louisville
Stacey Cade
Sacred Heart Model School, Louisville
Sister Catherine, O.S.U.
Sacred Heart Model School, Louisville
Judith Kelley Dolt
Gavin H. Cochran Elementary School,
Louisville
Elizabeth Dudley
Carrithers Middle School, Louisville
Jeanne Flowers
Sacred Heart Model School, Louisville
Karen Fowler
Carrithers Middle School, Louisville
Laura Hansen
Sacred Heart Model School, Louisville
Sandy Hill-Binkley
Museum of History and Science, Louisville
Deborah M. Hornback
Museum of History and Science, Louisville
Patricia A. Hulak
Newburg Middle School, Louisville
Rose Isetti
Museum of History and Science, Louisville
Mary Ann M. Kent
Sacred Heart Model School, Louisville
James D. Kramer
Gavin H. Cochran Elementary School,
Louisville
Sheneda Little
Gavin H. Cochran Elementary School,
Louisville
Brenda W. Logan
Newburg Middle School, Louisville
Amy S. Lowen*
Museum of History and Science, Louisville
Mary Louise Marshall
Breckinridge Elementary School, Louisville
Theresa H. Mattei*
Museum of History and Science, Louisville
Judy Reibel
Highland Middle School, Louisville
Pamela R. Record
Highland Middle School, Louisville
Margie Reed
Carrithers Middle School, Louisville
Donna Rice
Carrithers Middle School, Louisville
Ken Rosenbaum
Jefferson County Public Schools, Louisville
Edna Schoenbaechler
Museum of History and Science, Louisville

Karen Schoenbaechler
Museum of History and Science, Louisville
Deborah G. Semenick
Breckinridge Elementary School, Louisville
Dr. William McLean Sudduth*
Museum of History and Science, Louisville
Rhonda H. Swart
Carrithers Middle School, Louisville
Arlene S. Tabor
Gavin H. Cochran Elementary School,
Louisville
Carla M. Taylor
Museum of History and Science, Louisville
Carol A. Trussell
Rangeland Elementary School, Louisville
Janet W. Varon
Newburg Middle School, Louisville

MICHIGAN

Glen Blinn
Harper Creek High School, Battle Creek
Douglas M. Bollone
Kelloggsville Junior High School, Wyoming
Sharon Christensen*
Delton-Kellogg Middle School, Delton
Ruther M. Conner
Parchment Middle School, Kalamazoo
Stirling Fenner
Gull Lake Middle School, Hickory Corners
Dr. Alonzo Hannaford*
Western Michigan University, Kalamazoo
Barbara Hannaford
The Gagie School, Kalamazoo
Duane Hornbeck
St. Joseph Elementary School, Kalamazoo
Mary M. Howard
The Gagie School, Kalamazoo
Diane Hartman Larsen
Plainwell Middle School, Plainwell
Miriam Hughes
Parchment Middle School, Kalamazoo
Dr. Phillip T. Larsen*
Western Michigan University, Kalamazoo
David M. McDill
Harper Creek High School, Battle Creek
Sue J. Molter
Dowagiac Union High School, Dowagiac
Julie Northrop
South Junior High School, Kalamazoo
Judith O'Brien
Dowagiac Union High School, Dowagiac
Rebecca Penney
Harper Creek High School, Battle Creek
Susan C. Popp
Riverside Elementary School, Constantine
Brenda Potts
Riverside Elementary School, Constantine
Karen Prater
St. Joseph Elementary School, Kalamazoo
Joel Schuitema
Woodland Elementary School, Portage
Pete Vunovich
Harper Creek Junior High School, Battle
Creek
Beverly E. Wrubel
Woodland Elementary School, Portage

NEW YORK

Frances P. Bargamian
Trinity Elementary School, New Rochelle
Barbara Carter
Jefferson Elementary School, New Rochelle

Ann C. Faude
Heathcote Elementary School, Scarsdale
Steven T. Frantz
Heathcote Elementary School, Scarsdale
Alice A. Gaskin
Edgewood Elementary School, Scarsdale
Harriet Glick
Ward Elementary School, New Rochelle
Richard Golden*
Barnard School, New Rochelle
Seymour Golden
Albert Leonard Junior High School, New
Rochelle
Don Grant
Isaac E. Young Junior High School, New
Rochelle
Marybeth Greco
Heathcote Elementary School, Scarsdale
Peter C. Haupt
Fox Meadow Elementary School, Scarsdale
Tema Kaufman
Edgewood Elementary School, Scarsdale
Donna MacCrae
Webster Magnet Elementary School, New
Rochelle
Dorothy T. McElroy
Edgewood Elementary School, Scarsdale
Mary Jane Motl
Greenacres Elementary School, Scarsdale
Tom Mullen
Jefferson Elementary School, New Rochelle
Robert Nebens
Ward Elementary School, New Rochelle
Eileen L. Paolicelli
Ward Elementary School, New Rochelle
Donna Pentaleri
Heathcote Elementary School, Scarsdale
Dr. John V. Pozzi*
City School District of New Rochelle, New
Rochelle
John J. Russo
Ward Elementary School, New Rochelle
Bruce H. Seiden
Webster Magnet Elementary School, New
Rochelle
David B. Selleck
Albert Leonard Junior High School, New
Rochelle
Lovelle Stancarone
Trinity Elementary School, New Rochelle
Tina Sudak
Ward Elementary School, New Rochelle
Julia Taibi
Davis Elementary School, New Rochelle
Kathy Vajda
Webster Magnet Elementary School, New
Rochelle
Charles B. Yochim
Davis Elementary School, New Rochelle
Bruce D. Zeller
Isaac E. Young Junior High School, New
Rochelle

DENMARK

Dr. Erik W. Thulstrup
Royal Danish School of Educational Studies,
Copenhagen

*Trial test coordinators

Contents

Acknowledgments

Animal Defenses was developed at the Lawrence Hall of Science by Jean Echols during the mid-1970's. The author would like to thank Cary Sneider for his invaluable assistance during the final writing of this GEMS Teacher's Guide. Special thanks goes to Jefferey Kaufmann for designing the paper Tyrannosaurus rex, which continues to delight the many children who watch its huge silhouette move across their classroom wall.

Introduction

Through the ages, animals have had to protect themselves from the hungry jaws of predators. In the struggle for survival, a fascinating assortment of defense mechanisms, both structural and behavioral, have developed. These defenses range from the quiet camouflage of an insect on a blade of grass to the slashing horns of a Triceratops, protecting itself from the fierce attacks of a Tyrannosaurus rex.

This activity begins with a look at the defenses of dinosaurs. Only the defensive **structures** (sharp teeth, spikes, shields, horns, claws, and whip-like tails) are explored in the first part of the activity. Later, the focus moves to defensive **behaviors**, and examples are drawn from familiar animals of today. The children learn that dogs, cats, turtles, lizards, and other animals not only have some physical defenses similar to those of the dinosaurs, but also can protect themselves from hungry predators with a variety of behaviors, such as hiding quietly, running away, climbing a tree, or playing dead.

Animal Defenses is written for use with preschoolers and kindergarteners. You will find ideas for modifying and extending the activities for first and second graders on page 25. Special education classes have used this unit with great success. *Animal Defenses* is especially recommended for hearing-impaired and aphasic children because of the highly visual character of its activities.

Session 1: Dinosaur Defenses

Overview

The teacher introduces the concept of animal defenses by holding up dinosaur posters and asking the children to identify body parts that they think were used for protection. Then the teacher acts out a drama of a paper defenseless animal being pursued by a paper Tyrannosaurus rex. The defenseless animal needs teeth, claws, spikes, horns, and other defensive structures. Each student is given a precut defenseless animal and is asked to add paper features to protect the animal from Tyrannosaurus. The story continues when the teacher uses an overhead projector to portray huge images of the paper animals on the wall. The moving silhouettes of Tyrannosaurus and the children's animals, now equipped with imaginative defensive structures, add excitement and reinforce the concepts.

Time Frame

Teacher Preparation	30-45 minutes
Class Activities	
Teacher Introduces Defenses	5 minutes
The Drama of a Defenseless Animal	10 minutes
Children Add Defenses to Their Animals	15 minutes
The Drama of Animals with Defenses	15 minutes

What You Need

If your students do not use scissors, you will need only one large pair of scissors for precutting.

If your students cannot write their names, you will need only one pencil to write their names on the paper animals.

For each student:

☐ 1 pencil
☐ 1 4½" x 6" sheet of green construction paper for the defenseless animal
☐ 1 container of white paste or glue
☐ 1 pair of scissors

For the group:

☐ posters of Tyrannosaurus rex, Stegosaurus, and Triceratops (masters included on pages 17–19)
☐ patterns for cutouts:

• Defenseless animal (pattern A, master included on page 14)
• Tyrannosaurus rex (pattern B, master included on page 15)
• Volcano (pattern C, master included on page 16)

☐ 1 9" x 12" sheet of brown construction paper for Tyrannosaurus rex
☐ 2 9" x 12" sheets of green construction paper for the paper ferns
☐ 1 paper punch for making eyes
☐ 1 large pair of scissors for precutting
☐ 1 tray for the demonstration
☐ newspaper (enough to cover the work tables and the demonstration tray)
☐ 1 roll of transparent tape
☐ 1 overhead projector
☐ 1 projector screen, or light-colored wall (You can also use a large piece of white paper, at least 4' x 6', or a white cloth sheet and masking tape.)

(Optional) Making the Drama More Colorful:

The overhead projector is a delightful teaching tool, which adds drama and enthusiasm to the lesson. Children love seeing their creations as enormous silhouettes moving on the wall in front of them, and they learn from the experience. Using color in the drama adds beauty to the rapidly changing scenery, and makes Tyrannosaurus and the children's animals seem more real. If you wish to use colored overlays on the stage of an overhead projector, as described on pages 12–13, you will need:

☐ 1 12″ x 12″ sheet of dark blue transparent acetate or construction paper
☐ 1 3½″ x 3½″ sheet of yellow acetate or cellophane. (Folders made of colored acetate, available from most drug or office supply stores, are a good source of yellow and red acetate. You can also use clear acetate overlays, coloring them with markers designed for this purpose.)
☐ 1 2″ x 5″ sheet of red acetate or cellophane
☐ patterns for cut-outs (masters included on page 16)

● Moon (pattern D)
● Lava (pattern E)

Getting Ready

Preparing the Materials

1. Duplicate the patterns on pages 14–16 and cut out patterns A, B, and C.

2. Use pattern A to precut a defenseless animal for each child in your class and one for yourself:

   a. Cut green construction paper into 4½″ x 6″ rectangles.

   b. Place the pattern on top of four sheets of green paper (4½″ x 6″) and cut around the pattern. **Save the scraps for use in the class activity.**

   c. Use a paper punch to punch out eyes on the paper animals.

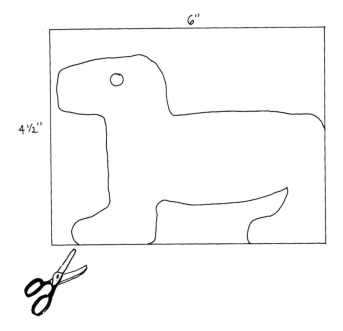

For students who do not use scissors, cut the scraps into triangles of different sizes. The children will use these shapes as tails, spikes, spines, teeth, nails, and horns to glue onto their defenseless animals. (Please see the drawing on page 9.)

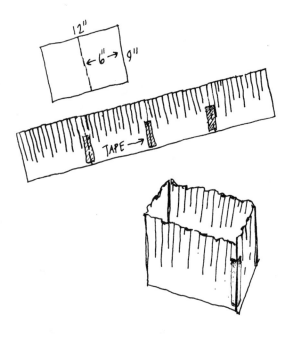

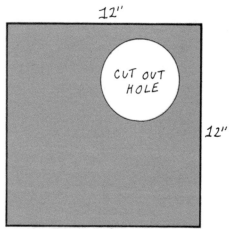

12"

CUT OUT HOLE

12"

BLUE ACETATE OR PAPER

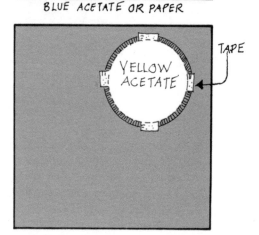

YELLOW ACETATE

TAPE

NIGHT SKY WITH A MOON

3. Use pattern B to cut Tyrannosaurus rex out of brown construction paper (9" x 12").

4. Pattern C, the Volcano, is used as a prop for a class activity. You do not need to cut it out of construction paper.

5. Make paper ferns:

    a. Cut two sheets of green 9" x 12" paper in half so that the cut pieces are 6" x 9".

    b. Place the four sheets on top of each other, and cut snips along one long side of the rectangle.

    c. Tape the four pieces of paper together at the short edges.

6. (Optional) To prepare a "Night Sky with a Moon":

    a. Cut out pattern D on page 16.

    b. Cut a circle (moon) with a 3" diameter out of the sheet of blue acetate or construction paper using pattern D.

    c. Cut a larger circle with a 3½" diameter out of the sheet of yellow acetate or cellophane.

    d. Tape the larger circle of yellow acetate over the hole in the blue acetate or construction paper.

7. (Optional) To prepare the hot lava, cut the lava shape out of the red cellophane using pattern E on page 16.

8. (Optional) Three 8½" x 11" posters are included in this unit. They may be used as is, or you may wish to have them enlarged at a photocopying shop.

Setting Up the Room

Arrange the room so there is a work area, a discussion area, and a place to set up the overhead projector and screen.

1. Prepare the Work Area. Spread newspaper on the tables. Place in each child's work area: paste, scissors, a pencil, a paper defenseless animal, and scraps of green paper (or triangular shapes) for tails, spikes, spines, teeth, nails, and horns.

2. Prepare the Discussion Area. During the class session, you will present a short play and demonstrate how to make a defenseless animal. Later, you will project the images of the paper animals on the wall. Arrange a section of the room so that the children are able to see these activities and participate in a discussion. Place in the discussion area:

- A tray for use in demonstrating how to add defenses to the paper animals. Place on the tray: newspaper, paste, scissors, a pencil, and paper scraps (or triangular shapes).

- Posters of Tyrannosaurus rex, Stegosaurus, and Triceratops.

- Paper props: defenseless animal, Tyrannosaurus rex, and ferns (made from green construction paper).

- Overhead projector.

- Screen (or white paper or sheet taped on wall).

- Paper volcano (pattern C) near the projector.

3. Place the overhead projector far enough from the wall so that the image size of the paper animals is quite large. Take time before you present the drama to practice manipulating the props on the stage of the projector.

4. (Optional) To make the drama more colorful, have the acetate sheet "Night Sky with a Moon" and the hot lava cutout near the projector.

You do not need scissors and pencils if you have already precut the animal defenses for your students and written their names on their animals.

Teacher Introduces Defenses

1. Gather the children in a circle on the floor in the discussion area. Explain to your students that many animals eat other animals, and all animals need to have ways to protect themselves. Tell the class that a long, long time ago in the days of the dinosaurs, dinosaurs needed to protect themselves from being eaten by other dinosaurs.

2. Show the poster of Stegosaurus. Ask, "What do you see on its back and tail that would stop other dinosaurs from trying to eat it?" [Plates on its back and spikes on its tail.]

3. Show the poster of Triceratops and have your students point out the parts of its body that they think were used for protection [horns and shield]. Tell the children, if they haven't already told you, that Tyrannosaurus rex and Triceratops lived at the same time and often fought fiercely with each other.

4. Show the poster of Tyrannosaurus and allow time for the children to share what they know about this famous monster. Ask, "How did Tyrannosaurus use its very large teeth?" [To eat other dinosaurs.] Explain that animals that lived at the same time as Tyrannosaurus needed to have many ways to protect themselves.

5. Tell your class that teeth, claws, horns, shields, spikes, and plates are called *defenses.* These defenses often saved animals from being eaten by other animals. Use the word "defenses" during the following activities.

The Drama of a Defenseless Animal

1. Tell the children they are going to see a play about a pretend animal that has no defenses: no teeth, no claws, no tail, no horns. It only has eyes.

2. Stand the paper ferns in the circle and hide the defenseless animal in the ferns.

3. Have the paper Tyrannosaurus rex walk around looking for something to eat. Tell the class that the hidden animal is safe as long as it stays very still, but, of course, it will get hungry. Before it can leave its hiding place to find food, it needs some way to protect itself.

4. Place the demonstration tray on the floor where the class can see it. As your students suggest a tail, claws, spikes, spines, shields, horns, and sharp teeth, cut out these defenses (or use precut ones) and glue them onto the defenseless animal, turning it into a scary creature.

5. Place the pretend animal back in its hiding place among the paper ferns. Have Tyrannosaurus return. Now the animal, protected with many defenses, can go out in search of food. Have it leave the ferns and walk around, while Tyrannosaurus stays at a safe distance.

Defenseless Animal

Animal with Defenses

Children Add Defenses to Their Animals

1. Instruct your students to go to their work places and write their names on their paper animals, if you have not already done so.

2. Encourage the children to add many defenses to their animals.

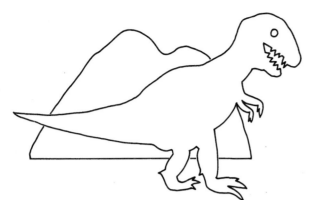

Tyrannosaurus passes a volcano.

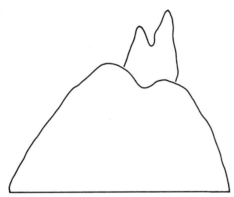

Hot lava slowly flows

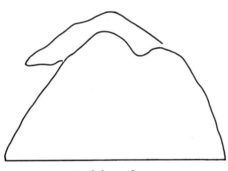

out of the volcano

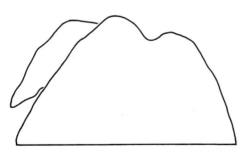

and down its side.

The Drama of Animals with Defenses

This drama is a performance of huge moving silhouettes of Tyrannosaurus rex and your students' paper animals. These characters seem to come alive as they walk across the screen. You place the paper animals, volcano, and night sky overlay (optional) on and off the stage of the overhead projector, while telling a story about Tyrannosaurus rex in search of food.

1. Gather the children in the discussion area. Place the paper Tyrannosaurus rex on the stage of the overhead projector and project it on the screen (or wall). Make up a story about Tyrannosaurus looking for food as you move the cutout across the stage. The story could go something like this:

   a. Tyrannosaurus is so hungry he walks all day searching for something to eat. He passes a volcano. (Place volcano on stage.)

   b. (Optional) Use the red cellophane shape to simulate hot lava slowly flowing out of the volcano and down its side.

   c. (Optional) It's night and a full moon rises. Still, Tyrannosaurus keeps looking for food. (Use the night sky overlay. Make Tyrannosaurus move through the night, his head silhouetted against the yellow moon.)

Tyrannosaurus moves through the night.

The sun comes up.

d. (Optional) A new day dawns. The sun comes up. (Remove the lava and the night sky overlay from the projector.)

e. Suddenly, on a distant hillside, Tyrannosaurus sees some animals. (Remove Tyrannosaurus rex and the volcano from the stage.)

An animal with many defenses

2. One at a time, project each child's animal on the screen. If possible, give each child an opportunity to tell the class about the defenses of his or her animal, as you move the animal across the stage of the projector. (If your class is too large to display each child's animal, choose only a few. During free time, the children can take turns projecting their own animals on the screen and making up stories.)

3. To show off the defenses on the tails, flick the back ends of the animals up and down to make it look as though they are whipping their tails. The whole animal does not have to be on stage at once.

whips its spiky tail.

4. Place Tyrannosaurus on the stage once again. Tell the class that Tyrannosaurus sees their animals, but he is not going to get near them because they have too many defenses.

Tyrannosaurus watches from far away.

PATTERN A, DEFENSELESS ANIMAL

PATTERN B, TYRANNOSAURUS REX

LHS—Great Explorations in Math and Science: *Animal Defenses*

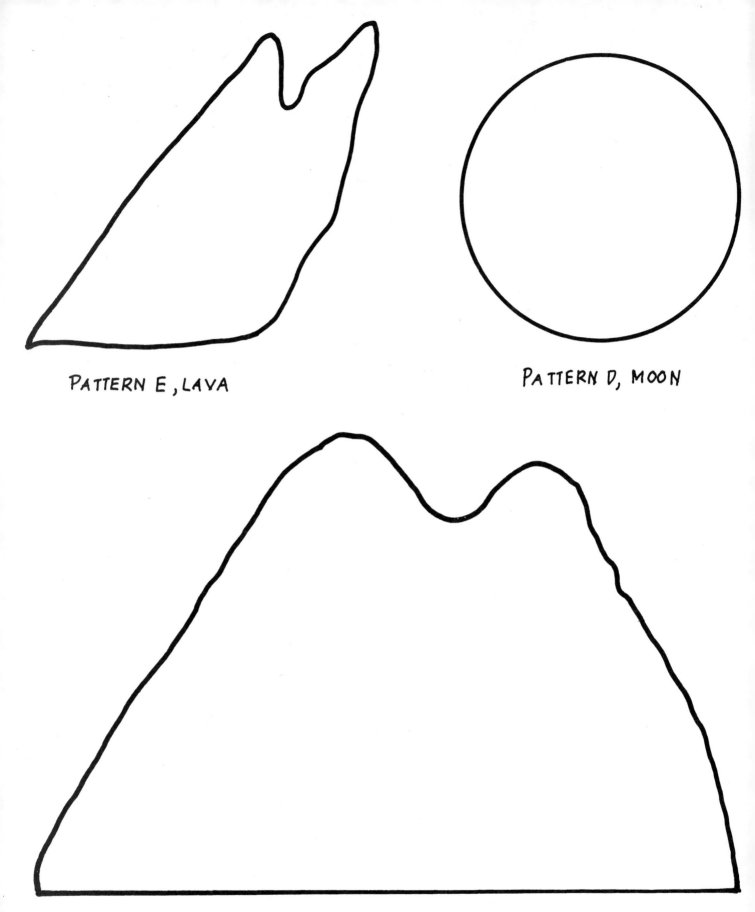

PATTERN E, LAVA

PATTERN D, MOON

PATTERN C, VOLCANO

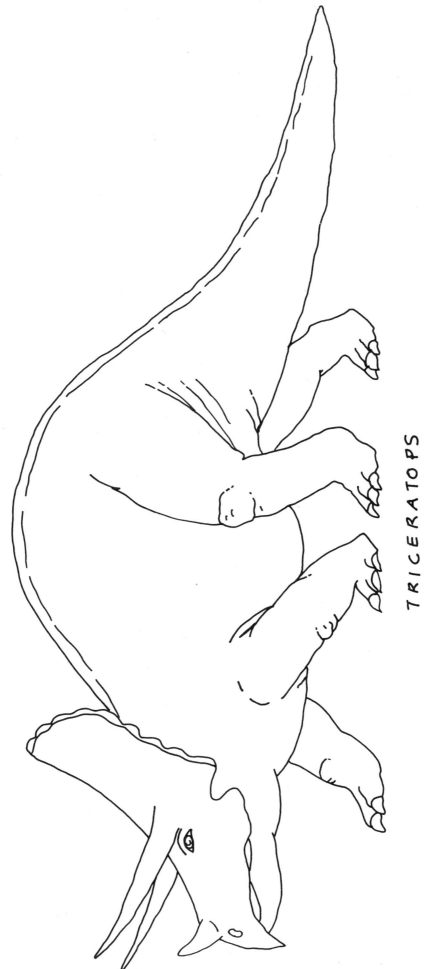

TRICERATOPS

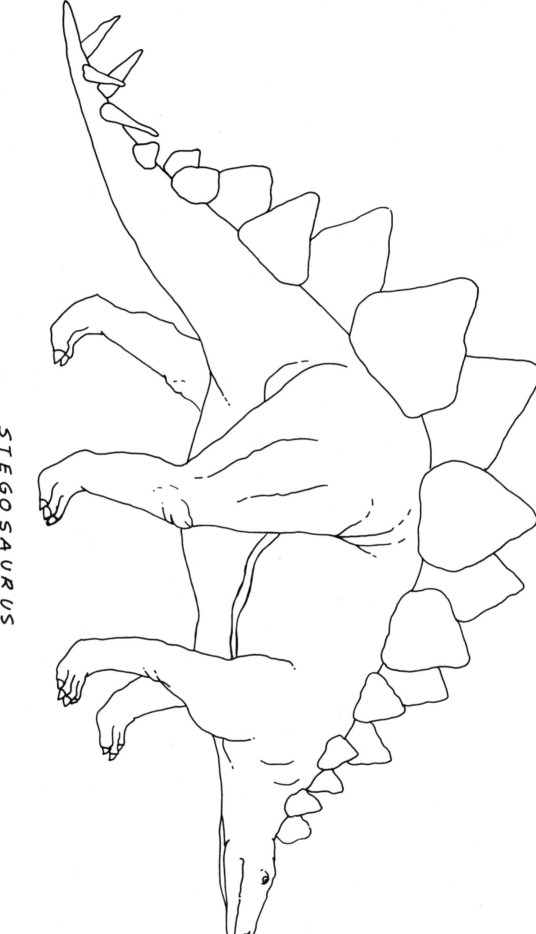

STEGOSAURUS

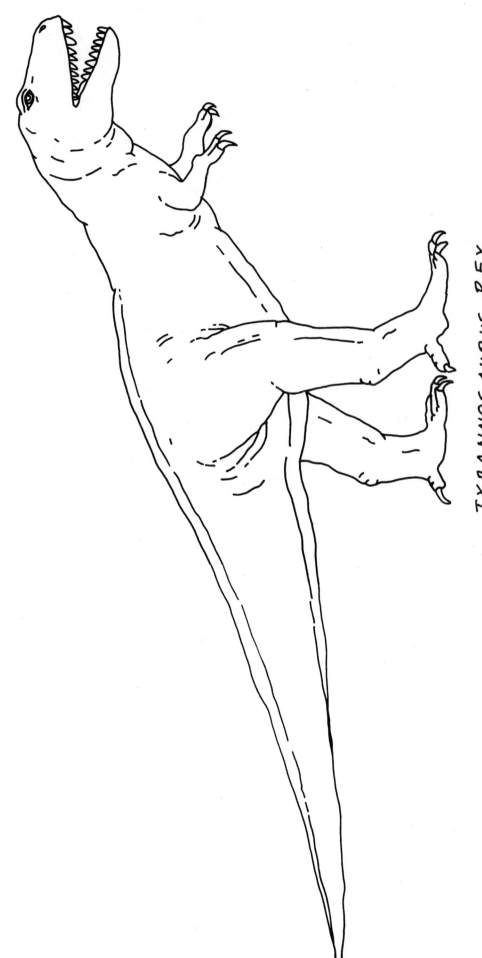

TYRANNOSAURUS REX

Session 2: Defenses of Animals that Live Today

Overview

In this session, the class takes a look at the defenses of animals that live today. The children learn that dogs, cats, turtles, lizards, and other animals not only **have** some physical defenses similar to those of the dinosaurs, but also can protect themselves from hungry predators by **doing** a variety of things, such as hiding quietly, running away, climbing a tree, or playing dead. Toy animals or photographs are used to help create stories that introduce the idea of defensive behavior.

Time Frame

Teacher Preparation	10–20 minutes
Class Activities	
Things Animals Have	10 minutes
Things Animals Do	10 minutes

What You Need

For the group:
- ☐ toy animals or large animal photographs representing animals that live today
- ☐ large color illustrations from dinosaur books
- ☐ 1 large paper bag

Getting Ready

1. Have your students bring dinosaur books with large, colorful illustrations from home or from a library.

2. Ask for volunteers to bring toy animals (preferably realistic looking ones) from home. The animals will be used to act out the behavior of animals that live today. If toys are not available, large color photographs of animals will do. Hide these toy animals or animal photographs in a large paper bag.

Things Animals Have

1. Gather the children in a circle on the floor in the discussion area and review dinosaur defenses, using illustrations from books about dinosaurs.

2. Tell your students that many of the animals that live today have defenses similar to those of dinosaurs.

3. Choose an animal that has sharp teeth (such as a rat) from the bag of toy animals or animal photographs. Have your students identify its defenses.

4. Select an animal that has sharp claws (cat), horns (bull), or a tail that is used as a whip (lizard). Allow time for the children to talk about the different defenses.

Things Animals Do

1. Choose a toy animal that eats other animals (cat). Introduce the idea of defensive behaviors by making up different scenarios for each animal that the cat encounters. The cat could meet up with a rat. Ask, "What do you think the rat would do?" [Bite, hide, run away.] Have the toy rat run away from the cat and hide.

2. Use other toys to act out animal behavior, or choose students to manipulate the toys as you talk. (Below is a list of animals and a list of the structures and behaviors that they use to defend themselves.)

3. Ask the children, "What are some of the ways you protect yourselves?" [Kick, run away, cover up in bed to hide.] You may want to add, "or you can even ask someone to please *not* do that."

If your students get mixed up between what animals do *and* have *for defense, give an example: Biting is what animals* do*. Teeth are what they* have *for defense.*

Animal	Things Animals Have	Things Animals Do
dog	teeth	growls, bites, runs away
cat	teeth, claws	bites, scratches, climbs
rat	teeth	bites, hides, climbs, runs away
deer	long legs	runs swiftly, kicks
bird	wings	flies away
turtle	hard shell	hides in its shell
skunk	odor glands	fans its tail as a warning, sprays
possum	teeth	bites, plays dead, climbs
lizard	teeth, tail, spines	bites, runs, hides, plays dead, whips with its tail, loses its tail and grows a new one, looks ferocious (some can blow themselves up to look larger)
butterfly	protective coloration, wings	remains perfectly still, flies away
bee	stinger, wings	stings, flies away

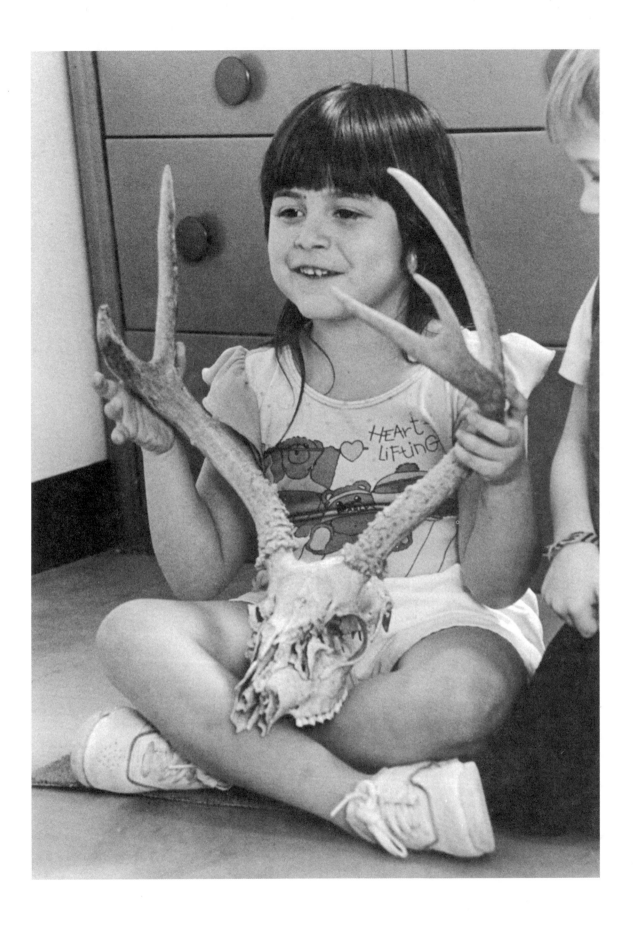

Extensions and Modifications for Grades 1 and 2

Session 1

- Students who are skilled with scissors can design their own defenseless animals, and then add spikes, shields, horns, claws, and teeth.

- Students can also make their own props with construction paper, and colored cellophane or acetate, to use with the overhead projector.

- As a language arts extension, your students can create their own dramas or short stories.

- Children who have good drawing and cutting skills can make their animals sturdier by using manila folders instead of construction paper.

- One teacher had her students make their animals into puppets by gluing on popsicle sticks to use as handles.

- If you use clay for art projects, your students can make their defenseless animals from clay, and add clay defenses.

Session 2

- Extend this session by having your students bring in toy animals each day for "show and tell" sessions. Focus short discussions on the animals' defenses.

- Have your students classify animals according to their defenses. Younger chidren can do this with toy animals or pictures of animals. Older children can list animals with sharp teeth, claws, tough skins, etc.

- For students in the first grade and older, introduce the words "predator" (an animal that hunts and eats other animals) and "prey" (an animal that is hunted and eaten). While you are using the toy animals or photographs to act out animal behavior, have your students identify the predator and the prey. Use these words often during the activity.

- Reinforce the predator-prey concept by having your children pair up to play the following art game: Each child draws an imaginary animal that could be prey. They then exchange papers and draw an imaginary predator that could eat that animal. They exchange papers a third time and draw what the prey might do, or add a structure it might need, to protect itself.

- Extend the predator-prey concept by introducing the idea that a predator may become prey to another animal. For example, a cat is the predator of rats and mice. But the cat can also be prey to a hawk or a wolf. The mouse, cat, and wolf are links in a *food chain.*

- Have your students make a diorama from a shoebox and construction paper. They draw and cut out predators and prey to create a food chain. They also make grass, shrubs, and trees to make a scene inside the box.

- Plan a field trip to the zoo following this unit. At the zoo, encourage your students to describe the defenses of the animals that they see.

Simon simon Simon simon

Mathematical Extensions

Before you begin, make picture/word labels for the following defenses: Tails, Claws, Spikes, Shields, Horns, Teeth. Also make sure the students' names are on their animals.

 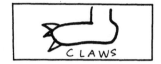 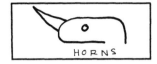 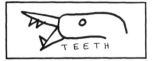

Use the following method to survey the class to determine how many children added particular defenses to their animals. Gather the children in a circle on the floor, with their animals. Make a statement that refers to each defensive structure, such as "Hold up your animal if you added a tail to it."

As you make the statement, place the label for "Tails" on one end of the circle. Ask a student to "read" the label by identifying the picture. Have the children place all animals that have tails in a line by the label. Count this number of animals with the class. Write the number on a piece of paper next to the label, i.e., "12 Tails."

Then have the children take back their animals. Continue the survey in the same manner with the other defenses, one at a time. Discuss the results as appropriate.

Grades 1–2

The defenses that students added to their animals can be graphed, using either beans in cylinders or small jars, or graph paper with dinosaur stickers or paper squares. To construct the graph, students place one bean in each of the cylinders (or one square on the graph) that is labelled with a defense that they placed on their animal. See illustration below.

When the graphs are completed, ask questions like the following:

- How many people added tails to their animals? spikes? teeth ?
- What defense did most people add ? What defense did the least people add?
- Were there more tails or teeth? Were there less claws or horns?

Students could also complete a sentence about their animal, such as

"My animal is protected because it has __ tails, __claws, ___ spikes, ___ spines, ___ shields, ___ horns and ___ teeth.

When the sentences are finished, you can play a game. Have four students volunteer their animals and sentences. Place the animals where all students can see them. Ask one student at a time to read her sentence describing her animal. Challenge classmates to identify which animal is hers. After you model the activity to make sure all students understand it, have them work in groups of four to play the game.

Summary Outlines

Session 1: Dinosaur Defenses

Teacher Introduces Defenses
1. Introduce need for protection.
2. Identify defenses on poster of Stegosaurus.
3. Identify defenses on poster of Triceratops.
4. Show poster of Tyrannosaurus, a meat-eater.
5. Define *defenses.*

The Drama of a Defenseless Animal
1. Introduce play of defenseless animal.
2. Hide animal in ferns.
3. Tyrannosaurus searches for food.
4. Add defenses to animal.
5. Show how defenses protect against Tyrannosaurus.

Children Add Defenses to Their Animals
1. Send the children to their work areas.
2. Have students add defenses to animals.

The Drama of Animals with Defenses
1. Gather students near overhead projector.
   a. Hungry Tyrannosaurus walks past volcano.
   b. Have lava flow from volcano.
   c. Tyrannosaurus walks through the night.
   d. The sun comes up.
   e. Tyrannosaurus sees the animals.
2. Project children's animals on screen.
3. Flick tails to show off defenses.
4. Tyrannosaurus stays away from animals.

Session 2: Defenses of Animals that Live Today

Things Animals Have
1. Review dinosaur defenses.
2. Today's animals have similar defenses.
3. Children identify defenses of toy animal with sharp teeth.
4. Children identify defenses of toy animals with other defenses.

Things Animals Do
1. Introduce idea of defensive behaviors using cat and rat.
2. Use other toys to act out defensive behaviors.
3. Ask the children to identify their own defensive behaviors.

Assessment Suggestions

Selected Student Outcomes

1. Students identify the defensive structures and behaviors that dinosaurs used to protect themselves.

2. Students apply their knowledge of defensive structures to create a model of a defended animal.

3. Students demonstrate their knowledge of the predator-prey relationship through dramatic play.

4. Students use their knowledge of prehistoric defenses to help them understand animal defenses in today's world.

Built-In Assessment Activities

Defense!

In Session 1, students see drawings of dinosaurs and then watch a drama about a defenseless animal. They are asked to identify body structures and behaviors that helped to defend the dinosaurs. During the drama, students are asked to name additional structures and behaviors that would help protect the defenseless animal. Throughout the session, teachers can listen to the students' responses; watch for rich, descriptive language and note their observations next to each student's name on a class list. (Outcome 1)

Make a Defended Animal

In Session 1, students design their own defended animal as they add paper horns, spines, teeth, and wings to a cutout defenseless form. The teacher circulates among the class, poses questions, and asks students to explain the decisions they made about their creatures. Student learning can be measured by their oral descriptions and the complexity and detail of their model. (Outcomes 1, 2)

Note: This activity is featured as a case study, with detailed analysis of actual student work, in *Insights and Outcomes: Assessments for Great Explorations in Math and Science*, also known as the GEMS assessment handbook, and available from GEMS.

Assessment Suggestions (continued)

My Animal in Action

In the final activity of Session 1, students use their defended animal in an action-packed confrontation with *Tyrannosaurus rex*. As they observe the dramatic play, the teacher can listen and assess the degree to which students are able to describe the animal's structures and behaviors, and how each defense functions as protection. (Outcomes 1, 3)

Animal Defenses Today

In Session 2, students create scenarios with toy animals to illustrate the structures and behaviors that protect animals common to today's world. These scenarios will illustrate whether students are able to generalize their knowledge about prehistoric defenses to help them understand animal defenses in their own world. (Outcome 4)

Additional Assessment Ideas

Once Upon a Time

During Session 1, students can write or dictate stories about their defended animal and then perform these stories for classmates and families. (Outcomes 1, 3)

Underwater Defenses

At the end of the unit, have students design a defenseless form of an animal that lives in water. Encourage them to add defenses and behaviors that would assist this animal in its underwater home. (Outcomes 1, 2, 3, 4)

Teachers are always suggesting new literature connections. One frequently recommended book for this unit is entitled *Animal Defenses: How Animals Protect Themselves* by Etta Kaner, Kids Can Press, Toronto, 1999.

Literature Connections

We welcome your suggestions for other books that make meaningful literature connections to *Animal Defenses.* The GEMS literature handbook, *Once Upon A GEMS Guide: Connecting Young People's Literature to Great Explorations in Math and Science*, includes many other excellent books related to science themes, mathematics strands, and all the other guides in the GEMS series.

Curious Clownfish
by Eric Maddern; illustrated by Adrienne Kennaway
Little, Brown & Co., Boston. 1990   *Grades: K–3*
> A baby clownfish wants to leave the protection of the anemone whose stinging tentacles he keeps clean. While exploring a coral reef he encounters a sea slug, porcupine fish, dragon fish, crab, cuttlefish, and a terrifying eel. They all demonstrate their defense mechanisms and he is grateful to return to the anemone. Illustrations depict a beautiful undersea world as well as showing defensive behaviors.

Dinosaurs are Different
by Aliki
HarperCollins, New York. 1985   *Grades: K–3*
> Explains how various orders and suborders of dinosaurs were similar and different in structure and appearance. A good catalogue of dinosaur defenses.

Dinosaurs, Dinosaurs
by Byron Barton
Thomas Y. Crowell, New York. 1989   *Grades: K–2*
> In prehistoric days there were many different kinds of dinosaurs, big and small, those with spikes and those with long sharp teeth. Perfect to read either before or after Session 1 of the GEMS guide.

Eric Carle's Animals Animals
compiled by Laura Whipple; illustrated by Eric Carle
Philomel/Putnam & Grosset, New York. 1989   *Grades: K–5*
> Anthology of over 50 poems from many cultures on both wild and domestic animals illustrated with joyous color collages. The poems cover a wide range of topics, and some, such as those on the barracuda, porcupine, and narwhal, focus particularly on animal defenses.

A House for Hermit Crab
written and illustrated by Eric Carle
Picture Book Studio, Saxonville, Massachusetts. 1987   *Grades: Preschool–2*
> One day Hermit Crab moves out of the house he has outgrown and finds a bigger shell "house" that is perfect but plain. He collects sea anemones, starfish, coral, snails, sea urchins, lantern fish, and pebbles to adorn it. When he outgrows that home, he finds a bigger one with new decorating possibilities—barnacles, clown fish, sand dollars, and electric eels. Text in front and back adds information about the crab's habitat and defenses used by other creatures.

Literature Connections (continued)

Lizard in the Sun
by Joanne Ryder; illustrated by Michael Rothman
William Morrow, New York. 1990   *Grades: Preschool–2*
> The friendly narration guides you through your day as a lizard; you are camouflaged from hungry birds and hidden from insects that become your next meal. Children enjoy seeing the natural world from a lizard's viewpoint, and learn firsthand facts about a lizard's lifestyle.

The Mixed-Up Chameleon
by Eric Carle
Harper & Row, New York. 1975   *Grades: Preschool–2*
> A bored chameleon wishes it could be more like all the other animals it sees, but soon decides it would rather just be itself. Protective coloration (the chameleon changes color according to the surface on which it rests) and energy (when the chameleon is warm and full, it turns one color, when cold and hungry, it turns another) are woven into the story.

Mousekin's Golden House
written and illustrated by Edna Miller
Prentice-Hall, Englewood Cliffs, New Jersey. 1964
Simon & Schuster, New York. 1987   *Grades: K–3*
> Mousekin acquires an unusual tool for self defense in the forest— a discarded jack-o-lantern in which he hides from a hungry young owl, a cat, and a box turtle. As the cut-out spaces in the pumpkin slowly melt together, he has an even cozier golden house.

Pretend You're A Cat
by Jean Marzollo; illustrations by Jerry Pinkney
Dial Books, New York. 1990   *Grades: Preschool–1*
> Wonderful illustrations and friendly verse ask children, "Can you chatter and flee? Disappear in a tree? Young readers can read the verse and act out the animal's behavior. Animals include a cat, pig, snake, bear, horse, and seal. Great springboard to a discussion of similarities and differences among animal behaviors.

Swimmy
by Leo Lionni
Alfred A. Knopf, New York. 1987   *Grades: K–4*
> A clever little black fish discovers a way for her school of little red fish to swim together and be protected from larger predators. With Swimmy as the "eye," the fish swim in formation masquerading as a big fish.